Allegro de Concierto, Capricho Español
and Other Works for Solo Piano

Enrique Granados

DOVER PUBLICATIONS, INC.
Mineola, New York

Bibliographical Note

This Dover edition, first published in 2002, is a new compilation of works originally published in authoritative early editions. English translations of the Spanish titles are newly added.

International Standard Book Number: 0-486-42429-4

Manufactured in the United States of America
Dover Publications, Inc., 31 East 2nd Street, Mineola, N.Y. 11501

CONTENTS

Allegro de Concierto, Capricho Español

and Other Works for Solo Piano

A la cubana

In Cuban style (Op. 36)

I.

D.C. al fine

II.

Un poco vivo

Coda
Primo tempo

Allegro de concierto

Concert allegro (Op. 46)

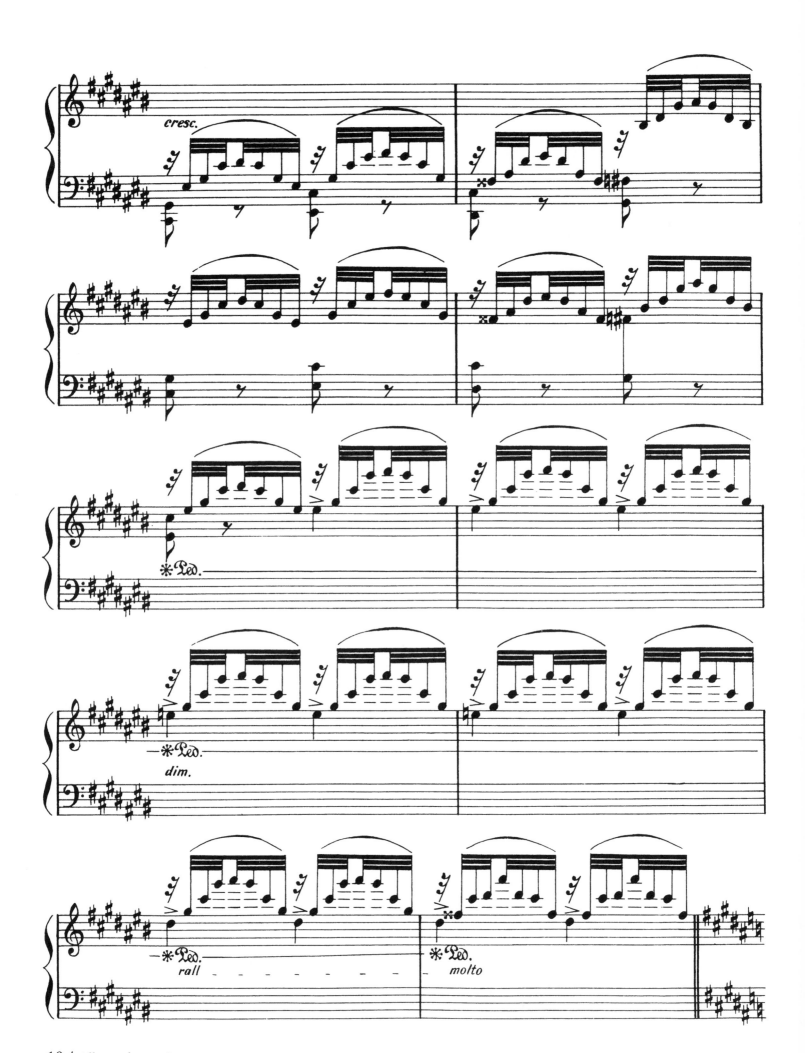

Allegro spiritoso

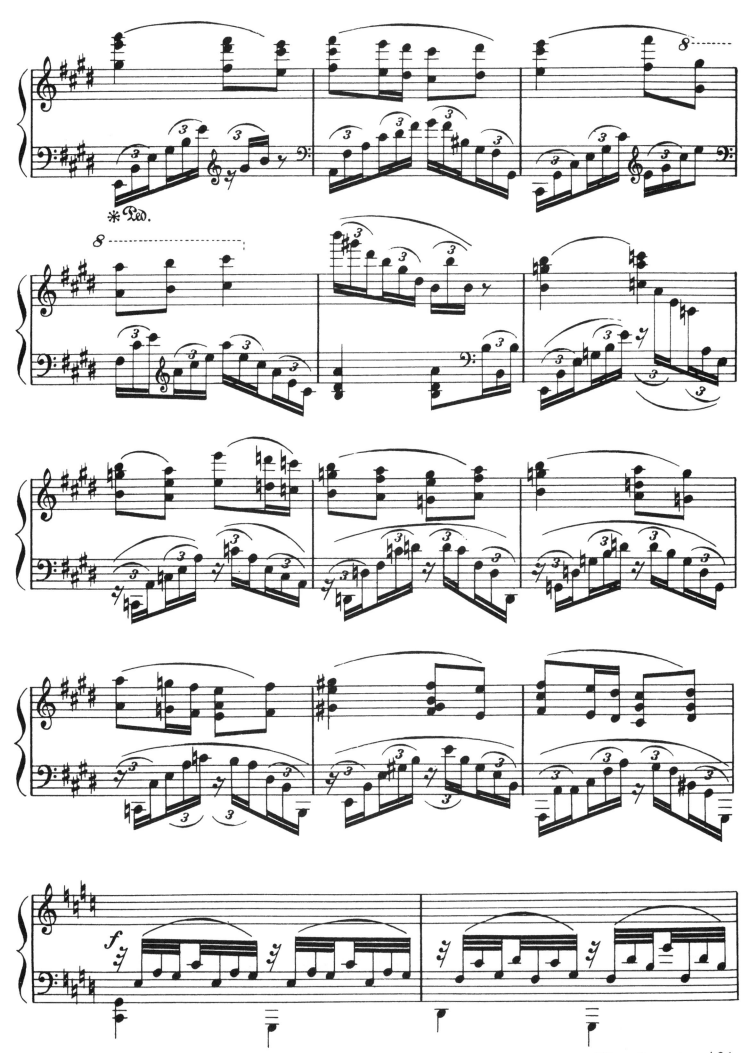

Capricho español

Spanish caprice (Op. 39)

Dos danzas españoles

Two Spanish dances (Op. 37)

à la mémoire de Vincente Esteve

I. Danza lenta
Slow dance

à Ernest Schelling

II. Sardana

Catalan dance: from *Two Spanish Dances* (Op. 37)

D.C.

Dos impromptus

Two impromptus

I.

Allegretto pastorale

Meno e con molta grazia

II. Impromptu de la codorniz

The quail's impromptu: from *Two impromptus*

à Enrique Montoriol Tarrés

El pelele

(Escena goyesca)

The puppet (after a painting by Goya)

Intermezzo

From the opera *Goyescas*

à ma Mère

Moresque

Moorish piece

Cancion arabe

Arabian song

Marche militaire
Military march (Op. 38)

Seis piezas
sobre cantos populares españoles

Six pieces on Spanish folksongs

Preludio

I. Añoranza

Longing: from *Six pieces on Spanish folksongs*

Con moto

II. Ecos de la parranda

Echos of the celebration: from *Six pieces on Spanish folksongs*

III. Vascongada

In Basque style: from *Six pieces on Spanish folksongs*

IV. Marcha oriental

Oriental march: from *Six pieces on Spanish folksongs*

sempre dim.

v. Zambra

Moorish dance: from *Six pieces on Spanish folksongs*

VI. Zapateado

Stamping dance: from *Six pieces on Spanish folksongs*

Poco meno (Scherzo)

ZAPATEADO

Tempo Iº

Ochos valses poeticos

Eight poetic waltzes

110

Tempo de Valse noble

2.

rubato *rall.* *a tempo*

dim. *con molta fantasia* **pp** *rit.* *vivo* **pp**

cresc.

rubato

Adagio **pp**